COMEDY AND DARKNESS POETRY

By

Carol Monroe

First published in April 2024 by Carol Monroe.

Copyright © Carol Monroe 2024

Carol Monroe has asserted her rights under 'the Copyright Designs and Patents Act 1988' to be identified as the author of this work.

All rights reserved.

No part of this document may be reproduced or transmitted in any form or by any means, electronic, mechanical, photocopying, recording, or otherwise, without prior written permission of the Author.

DEDICATION

This poetry book is dedicated to all the special people in my life who have made me laugh and supported me throughout 2023.

You all know who you are.

Comedy and Darkness Poetry

Other books by Carol Monroe:

HEARTBREAK AND DARKNESS POETRY

MENTAL HEALTH AND DARKNESS POETRY

COMEDY, HEARTBREAK AND MENTAL HEALTH POEMS

Comedy and Darkness Poetry

To All the People

To all the people who made me smile and be happy

To all the people who made me stronger unknowingly

To all the people who I have not met yet

You will be in one of my books, I bet!

Comedy and Darkness Poetry

Comedy and Darkness Poetry

ACKNOWLEDGEMENTS

Comedy and Darkness Poetry

Comedy and Darkness Poetry

ACKNOWLEDGEMENTS

A special mention goes to a friend from my old radio days, my co-presenter DJ Hevsta. Thank you for keeping an eye on me during 2023, and for being my 'back up buddy'! Thanks for listening to me, you are a life saver.

A big thank you goes to my friend Peter for supporting me and listening to me. I am always grateful for you making lots of Earl Grey tea. I have always appreciated your advice too.

A special thank you goes to Paula and Matt for always being there for me for all these years. Paula inspired me years ago to start writing a book. I remember when she handed a book to me and told me, ***"You can write better than that! You need to write a book."***

Comedy and Darkness Poetry

Paula is like a sister to me, and for those who know me well, you will know how much that means to me.

A big thank you goes to my old school friend Mike. Thank you for giving me material to write about. Mike and I have been friends since we were twelve years old. I am sure he will return in other poems at some point involving funny stories that have happened in my life!

Thank you to Sharon and Dave for being such amazing and supportive friends for so many years. Plus, thanks for always feeding me when I come to your house! Sharon, I will write a proper poem about you one day, I promise!

To Ros, thank you so much for all the years you have spent with me, drinking coffee in Blakes.

Comedy and Darkness Poetry

Plus, thanks for giving me a reason to write yet another poem! We have always gone to Blake's to grab a cuppa and have some deep conversations. I hope that we have lots more coffee and poems in the future!

A final thank you goes to Alan and The Spire Art Café staff in Gateshead. I wrote some of the poems in this book in the café, so I must give the place a special mention in this book. Thank you for providing so many smiles, vegetarian breakfasts, cups of coffee and Earl Grey tea!

Carol Monroe

Comedy and Darkness Poetry

Comedy and Darkness Poetry

CONTENTS

Comedy and Darkness Poetry

Comedy and Darkness Poetry

CONTENTS

Introduction	1
The Poems	7
Comedy and Darkness	9
Stealing My Socks	11
Clarice	13
Viking Blood	14
MOT Fail	15
The Con Man and The Lady	18
Chrissy Rock in the Loos	20
Your Face on TV	23
The Journey from Lanzarote	24
Coniston Lake	30
Buffalo Bill with Frosted Pink Lipstick & 10 Denier Tights	37
Blake's in Town and the Killing Joker	41
Ain't Nobody Got Time for That	44
Lalo and Tuco	46
It was a Dark Damp Night	47

Comedy and Darkness Poetry

The Limericks 49

Dawn 51

Maureen and Dawn 51

A Singer called Dave 52

A Guitarist called Anton 52

A Comedian called Dawn 53

A Girl Called Carol 53

Maraca Knacker 54

The Mechanic 55

A Lady Called Trish 55

A Goddess Called Sue 56

A Lady Called Brenda 56

A Guy Called Mick 57

A Girl Called Caz 57

A Woman Called Sharon 58

Mew and Andrew 58

Dawn and her Comedy Manager 59

Bob the Plumber 60

Comedy and Darkness Poetry

Lalo and Tuco at the Barista Boho	62
Two Chihuahuas	63
A Guy Called Kirk	63
A Girl Called Paula	64
My Friend Called Mike	64
A Guy Called Peter	65
Paula's Dad	66
A Dog Called Rosco	66
About the Poems	67
About the Limericks	79
Other Books	89
The Author	97

Comedy and Darkness Poetry

Comedy and Darkness Poetry

INTRODUCTION

Comedy and Darkness Poetry

Comedy and Darkness Poetry

INTRODUCTION

I have always written poetry throughout my life, and I've enjoyed writing my poems. However, I have never previously given any thought into putting together a selection of poems in the form of a book. I had never considered that other people may be interested in reading my poems, and gain something from reading them.

I had originally decided to write a different kind of book about my real life hilarious past situations. However, events occurred in 2023, which meant that I had to change my path slightly. So, I decided to do a short poetry book instead. Then that grew to three short poetry books on three different subject matters.

My Comedy and Darkness Poetry book is based

Comedy and Darkness Poetry

on real life situations that I have found myself in, or friends of mine that have been in these situations. The main feature of this first book is around comedy and funny events. There is also a touch of darkness as it incorporates real life.

There are so many hilarious events described in a rhyme form, which makes the situations sound even funnier! Last year, I started to write a bit of comedy poetry. It started with writing funny poems to make people laugh.

I had also started to write little bits of funny poetry to cheer myself up. Then, this year, I decided to publish my work. It would be a shame not to share my funny stories to the world! There are certain poems in this book that do not need an explanation.

Comedy and Darkness Poetry

More events occurred within these true tales, but for the purposes of entertainment, I kept to the funny stuff!

There are poems in this book that are a little bit vague on purpose. I am talking about certain people, but their names will never be revealed. I am sure that these poems will still hold some meaning for people, by how the reader interprets them.

There is always some kind of comedy to be found in our everyday lives, and I hope that I will brighten up your day with the funny poems in this book.

I also hope that the darker side of my poetry resonates with people. Life is full of ups and downs, and I hope that this book reflects this in a small way.

Comedy and Darkness Poetry

There are a few slightly naughty words within some of the poems, so I am giving you advanced warning now. If you hear me perform any of my poems live, the rude words get slightly worse!

I must give a special mention to the lyrical genius of punk poet laureate John Cooper Clarke. He got lots of regular airplay on a local community radio show that I did for around 20 years in Newcastle upon Tyne.

I would like to think that I have taken a tiny bit of inspiration from him. He fitted in well with the punk rock, synth pop and new wave music content of the show, along with the silly comedy banter with my co-presenter Hevsta. Happy days!

At the end of this book there are several limericks to keep the giggles going.

Comedy and Darkness Poetry

If you are looking for a chuckle and a bit of entertainment, then this is the book for you! I have enjoyed writing the comedy poetry so much, I am sure that I will tell more tales in poetry form about my adventures in my lifetime.

So, look out for more comedy poetry books soon. I do believe that laughter and comedy can help with our mental health. Let's face it we all love a good giggle and good story telling.

These real life adventures will give you a glow inside and they will give you a few laughs too! I hope that you enjoy reading the forty stories in a comedy style in my first poetry book!

All the poems are snap shots in time and not a true reflection of who or where I am today. If you enjoy observational comedy, you will really enjoy reading this book!

Comedy and Darkness Poetry

I have written another two poetry books called Heartbreak and Darkness Poetry & Mental Health and Darkness Poetry. So, feel free to check those books out.

If you live in the North East of England, you might catch me in the future performing the odd poem or two, in a café or an open mike night.

Carol Monroe

Comedy and Darkness Poetry

THE POEMS

Comedy and Darkness Poetry

COMEDY AND DARKNESS

This book is about comedy and darkness
My wit and rhyme I wanted to harness

It's a new beginning, like a baby's birth
I decided to share some hilarious mirth

Without wanting to sound like a jackanory
I wanted to share some of my life story

I'm providing you with my funny wisdom
I needed to get it out of my system

I'm often described as happy and chirpy
Who knew this book would turn into therapy

Comedy and Darkness Poetry

So, flick through the pages and take a look

At all the stories in this book

I have plenty of stories stored in my mind

Buy the next book and you will find

More amazing stories that are true

They make me smile - I hope you will too!

Comedy and Darkness Poetry

<u>STEALING MY SOCKS</u>

Why are you so obsessed with my socks?
Look there's another one inside your toy box!

You look so pleased when you run away
Haha! You say, it's another payday!

Another sock for your collection
Oh, and did I forget to mention

Your partner in crime has a sneaky intention
To distract his mum and divert her attention

I sigh in despair when I look at my dog
He stares back at me with his eyes all agog

Comedy and Darkness Poetry

Yes, he has been caught in the act
With both dogs deciding to make a sock pact!

They think they're so clever when they both run away
I shake my head and sigh in dismay

This is now starting to get out of control
I can't find one sock without a hole!

Comedy and Darkness Poetry

CLARICE

Clarice you cannot save all the lambs
Or all of the children in the northeast prams
Clarice you are an angel it is clear to see
You help people with empathy and your spirituality

You cannot save all the lambs Clarice
Your kindness is glowing, it will never cease
You can wake the lambs up one by one
But sooner or later they will all be gone

For the wolves they circle around the doors
Of this I am certain, it cannot be ignored
You cannot save all the lambs Clarice
If you only save one, it may give you some peace

Comedy and Darkness Poetry

VIKING BLOOD

His hair is long, a strawberry blond
His tarot card is the Ace of Wands
He must have Viking in his blood
He can throw an axe hard into wood

He knows the art of self-defence
You will never find him on the fence
He makes his opinions known with no fear
He knows his own mind that's quite clear

He's a known master of Taoism you see
He's studied the works of Edgar Cayce
A friend that knows his own mind
Another bestie like Mike I will never find

Comedy and Darkness Poetry

<u>MOT FAIL</u>

Today was a very unusual day
A change of events suddenly came my way

Helpful friends looked after me
A change of plans to make me happy

My car had failed it's MOT
A sad event, I think you'll agree

The failure list looked like War and Peace
Time to say goodbye and finally release

A car that meant so much to me
To fix it would cost too much money

Comedy and Darkness Poetry

It was a shame to see a good car go
Can I cope without a car? I don't know

A phone call came from far away
That changed my mind without delay

A friend of mine had so much to say
The main message was "don't give it away!"

I decided to put in the effort to fix it
I took a chance and decided to risk it

I needed to cash in my holiday euros
To fix up my car and fix up my woes

It is now sitting in a far away garage
I have no idea how much they will charge

Comedy and Darkness Poetry

Will my car get back on the roads
I just don't know what the future holds

Today was a very unusual day
Blessed to have friends helping out this way

Failing an MOT is pretty shit
But my message for you is do not quit!

Comedy and Darkness Poetry

THE CON MAN AND THE LADY

Con man, con man, where can you be?

Hiding from a victim or waiting for me

Con man, con man, what did you say?

Anything at all to get your own way

Con man, con man, why did you lie?

People thought you were a good guy

Con man, con man, how is it so?

You took my confidence and my dough

Comedy and Darkness Poetry

Con man, con man, get off my handbag

He's taken the money, he's taken the swag

Con man, con man, you took my life savings

My money has gone due to him misbehaving

Con man, con man, why can't you see?

You'll get locked up and they'll throw away the key

Con man, con man, I plead and I beg

Give my money back or I will break your legs!

Comedy and Darkness Poetry

CHRISSY ROCK

Tonight, I got a bit of a shock

As I bumped into Chrissy Rock

I was stood there in the loo

While she was stood rifling through

A red basket by the toilet window

What was she doing? I don't know!

She was holding up a sanitary pad

This lady looked like she was mad!

Comedy and Darkness Poetry

I asked her if she was **"on the rob"**

She said **"no - it's the act - it's for my job!"**

It truly was a sight to see

And I think you will all agree

So, I asked to take a picture of her

She looked amazing you will concur

Later she roasted me in her show

I was pleased I sat in the front row

She said I **"looked like an extra from Cocoon"**

I laughed so hard - I was over the moon!

Comedy and Darkness Poetry

She was one of the best comics that I've seen

She truly is the Comedy Queen!

Some comedians could learn a thing or two

By that marvellous lady I met in the loo!

She may be a lady of such a small stature

But no other comedian could ever match her

We said goodbye as we were leaving

Which was rather hard as it was heaving

She is the best of the best with her wit

But most of all she takes no shit!

Comedy and Darkness Poetry

YOUR FACE ON TV

I can't seem to get away from your face
Some people would say it's a huge disgrace

You turn up unannounced on my tv screen
With your slicked back hair full of brill cream

A shadow of your former self
The TV shows dust you off from the shelf

You should be left inside your box
I'm tired of hearing of your life's hard knocks

Please sod off, I have no respect
For the crimes you committed what do you expect?

Comedy and Darkness Poetry

THE JOURNEY FROM LANZAROTE

It was time to go home at the end of the holiday
It was a quiet one on the beach in the bay

My transfer to the airport, well, it didn't turn up
I dialled the transfer number – the man was very abrupt

I heard him declare, ***"You've got the wrong day!"***
"I beg your pardon. What did you say?"

"You sent an email to my hotel."
"You are lying to me - this I can tell!"

Comedy and Darkness Poetry

"Well, there is no record of it in my book."
I told him ***"Get glasses, take another look!"***

"Well get a taxi and claim back the money."
"Check in shuts in 10 minutes. Are you being funny?"

So off to the taxi rank I dashed
"Driver is there any way you can please drive fast?"

"Vamos, Vamos, Vamos Por Favor!"

"Extra Euros in it for you I can assure!"

I got there on time - I flew through the doors
I skidded and tripped up onto the floor

Comedy and Darkness Poetry

I went through the scanner, naturally I was searched
Got called over by Security, he was sat on his perch

"Liquids in bags! Liquids in bags - must be separate!"
I swear this man was in such a state

"Do yooooo speeeeak EEEEnglish?" the Security man asked
What am I doing trying to pass this test?

"Better than you!" I loudly state
"Back of the queue!" were his words filled with hate

Comedy and Darkness Poetry

He barked at me whilst blowing a gasket
I took all my things back out of the basket

I didn't go to the back of the queue
He doesn't get to tell me what to do

By this time I was acting a little shady
As I pushed in front of a friendly lady

I couldn't be bothered with that red faced tit
I was sick and tired of all of his bullshit

I went through the scanner - the alarms went off again
This is starting to feel like such a pain

Comedy and Darkness Poetry

The Security lady touched me up
She lifted my cap and checked out my 'pups'

"Do it again, I rather like it" I say
She smiled and laughed loudly – she'd had a bad day

How on earth I didn't get arrested there
With my cheeky demeanour and 'devil may care'

I really must stop taking the piss
How on earth did it ever come to this?

I must behave, I take this on board
I don't want to be on 'Banged Up Abroad'

Comedy and Darkness Poetry

One of these days I will run out of luck

But I really don't care or give a flying 'duck'

Comedy and Darkness Poetry

CONISTON LAKE

It was a gorgeous, lovely summer's day

The four of us decided to get away

Off to Coniston Lake we went

The weather was awesome, it was heaven sent

We arrived next door to the boating club

We set up the tents then we went to the pub

We hobbled back home giggling all of the way

This was going to be a hilarious holiday

The next morning, we cooked breakfast oats

We grabbed our things and secured the boat

Comedy and Darkness Poetry

A fibreglass boat, whose name was Herbie
Bought from a man north-east of Kirby

The guys, they decided to swim the lake
Which, by the by was a stupid mistake

Off the guys went enjoying themselves
We stayed at the lake's edge, sunning
ourselves

Oh, how lovely, isn't that nice
A boat passes by offering the guys some advice

Suddenly, they swim a lot faster
Little did we know they were headed for disaster

Comedy and Darkness Poetry

They eventually reached the end of the lake
Why wouldn't they stop waving, for pity's sake

They jumped up and down, shouting and waving
Why do they continue this misbehaving?

Eventually we heard them starting to yelp
Eventually we heard the loud cries for help

"I think they need saving" I heard myself say
"Quick grab the boat - come let's away"

We dragged the boat out with both of the oars
We scraped the boat along the pebbly lake shore

Comedy and Darkness Poetry

The guys had stopped jumping up and down
It was time to change direction of those frowns

It took a while to row across the lake
"Oh, why are we doing this for God's sake?"

"We've been told there's huge 6-foot pike!"
Shouts the 18 stone rugby player called Mike

"The pike are huge, and they like to bite!"
I replied, ***"That boat person has been talking shite!"***

"I don't think the boat will take your weight guys"

Comedy and Darkness Poetry

"Maybe this decision wasn't so wise"

Mike replied, ***"We will just take it slow"***
"Pass over the oars, it's my turn to row"

So, back across the lake we go
Even though the boat sank in the lake so low

I took a look at what was under my sole
I found out that the boat had a great big hole

It must've been caused by a big sharp pebble
That's what I get for being a rebel

There's a lot of water inside this small ship
My confidence in it was starting to dip

Comedy and Darkness Poetry

I decided I should use my moccasin shoe
To bail out the water – what else could I do?

I told the guys ***"Row faster – keep rowing!"***
I glanced at my feet and the hole was growing

"I'm scared of dark water!" I shouted to my friends
I never imagined this was how my life ends

We eventually get to about halfway
With bailing and rowing, there was nothing to say

This part of the holiday was never planned
Only a few metres left till we get to dry land

Comedy and Darkness Poetry

Yay! We made it – then collapsed in a heap
We needed a breather before the boat went on the jeep

So, six-foot pike with great big teeth!
It's a crazy story no one will believe

Comedy and Darkness Poetry

BUFFALO BILL WITH FROSTED PINK LIPSTICK & 10 DENIER TIGHTS

Let me tell you about Mr 10 Denier Tights
I was walking away from the cinema one night

An event occurred which gave me a fright
A freaky flasher came into my sight

I had gone out that night with three work friends
What happened next, I still cannot comprehend

As I was approaching the door of my car
I saw a naked man jump over a bar

He headed towards us - his motives unknown
He was a little excited by what he was showing

Comedy and Darkness Poetry

He had his hand placed firmly on his groin
I didn't dare look at the rest of his loins

I couldn't get over his shade of lipstick
He was probably upset I didn't notice his 'wick'

It was a curious shade of frosted pink
The kind of colour to make the boys wink

Then I thought, this doesn't seem right
Why is he wearing 10 Denier Tights?

I stood stone still at the edge of the pavement
I saw the veins in his legs to my amazement

All the girls screamed at me – ***"Get in the car!"***
"He's coming closer – he's not very far"

Comedy and Darkness Poetry

I couldn't stop laughing, I found it so funny
Were they really TAN tights or were they HONEY?

I speeded away as he was coming closer
"State of him! He's such a poser!"

"Go to the police station and make a statement, please!"
In the background I hear my workmates tease.

I stopped at the local Jesmond telephone box
The police must've thought I was off my rocks

So off to the station I proceeded to go
What the hell do I tell them? I don't know

Comedy and Darkness Poetry

The lady PC said, *"OMG it's Tights Man!"*
I said, *"I do believe the shade of tights was TAN!"*

The lady PC gasped aloud:
"Our PC Willis will be so very proud"

"He's waited three months to apprehend this man!"
"He's on his way over to catch him if he can!"

I never found out about the aftermath
Did the police catch up with this psychopath?

It's been a while since I saw Buffalo Bill.
But those memories have stayed with me still.

Comedy and Darkness Poetry

BLAKES IN TOWN AND THE KILLING JOKER

It was Sunday when I went to Blake's in town
It was time to turn my frown upside down

I was meeting up with my friend Ros
She talked of her mother and brother in Oz

We had so much to catch up on and discuss
that day
We would never run out of things to say

Ros offered to buy me another drink
The waiter came over and he made me think

He looked over at me and I noticed his tee shirt

Comedy and Darkness Poetry

Should I ask about it? Well, it wouldn't hurt

"Is that a butterfly with a skull?" I asked
This waiter guy was not flummoxed

"Yes, it's from the Silence of the Lambs film"
Well, I am pleased I started talking to him

"I've just written a poem called Buffalo Bill!"
"I love a bit of darkness about people who kill"

I said, ***"What did you think of how Dexter ended?"***

Comedy and Darkness Poetry

He replied, ***"Beyond Season 5 is not recommended"***

He asked about the name of my poetry book
I think he was going to take a little look

"It has no name yet - do you have a suggestion?"
"The Killing Joke" was his recommendation!

It was lovely to chat to Ros that day
And the interesting stranger who I met on the way

I enjoyed my Blake's coffee and all the chat
The waiter is in this poem – I think he'd like that!

Comedy and Darkness Poetry

AIN'T NOBODY GOT TIME FOR THAT!

There was a lovely lady who loved to organise
One day she woke up and to her surprise

Had to deal with silly unreasonable folk
It has started to get beyond a joke!

She gives and gives till her cup runs dry
She looked perplexed and gave out a loud sigh

"Why am I entertaining all of this?"
"These people are starting to take the piss!"

She runs around, she runs around ragged
She won't tolerate another old haggard

Comedy and Darkness Poetry

Who has the folly to disturb her day
In the end karma will have to pay

"Ain't nobody got time for that!
Stop acting like a stupid prat!"

"Don't even pretend to be angry or shocked-
Disrespect me again and you will get
blocked"

Some people might start feeling a little bit miffed
She's starting to feel like Taylor Swift!

Darkening her door is unwise and wrong
She will name and shame you in a poem or song!

Comedy and Darkness Poetry

LALO AND TUCO

Lalo and Tuco are my two best friends
The laughs we have just never end

Tuco is cute, vicious and strong
With him by my side, I will never go wrong

Tuco is funny, cheeky and kind
A more handsome dog you will never find

Lalo is softer, peaceful and calm
He loves to cuddle in under my arm

Lalo's ears are amazingly massive
A character so sweet and incredibly passive

They are both so happy running around
I'm so blessed by the two dogs that I've found

Comedy and Darkness Poetry

IT WAS A DARK DAMP NIGHT

It was a dark, damp and dingy night

When the witches come out to give us a fright

We sat laughing in the Barista Boho

With Dean dressed up as Edgar Allan Poe

We cackled away as we stirred our pots

I was told to write a poem and I gave it a shot

Spells were cast to manifest a raven

Angela brought the raven with Anton

misbehaving!

Comedy and Darkness Poetry

My coven and I, we had a fabulous night

The great talent on show shone like a bright light

My minion (my dog) was too tired to take part

He's busy bringing joy and breaking hearts….

Comedy and Darkness Poetry

THE LIMERICKS

Comedy and Darkness Poetry

Comedy and Darkness Poetry

LIMERICK SECTION

DAWN

There was a comedian called Big Cat Banter

Who always drank cans of Fanta

We made her some coffee

When she ate all the toffee

Now she's off like a horse on a canter!

MAUREEN AND DAWN

At the Barista Boho take a seat

As Maureen read's out tales of Alien Pete

She does a double act

With her daughter in fact

A talented pair you should meet!

Comedy and Darkness Poetry

A SINGER CALLED DAVE

There was a singer called Dave

Who met a girl called Miss Behave

When he became flirty

Her chat was so dirty

It's a shame he needed a shave

A GUITARIST CALLED ANTON

There was a guitarist called Anton

Who was very fond of a scone

Angela had baked all day

With her back turned away

Anton scoffed them till they were all gone!

Comedy and Darkness Poetry

A COMEDIAN CALLED DAWN

I know a comedian called Dawn

Who always looked quite forlorn

She said ***"Listen Caz, honey"***

"You are not that funny"

As she responds to my jokes with a yawn!

A GIRL CALLED CAROL

There was a girl called Carol

Who felt as round as a barrel

She told jokes that were funny

That made her some money

All the folks in the audience would howl!

MARACA KNACKER

Caz was a bit of a cracker

Who broke someone else's maraca

She was so enthusiastic

As she thought they were plastic

Now she's known as the maraca knacker!

Caz can't be trusted with maracas

Whatever she touches she knackers

It was really no joke

When one went up in smoke

She could smash your Jacob's Crackers!

Comedy and Darkness Poetry

THE MECHANIC

My MOT failure list was problematic

That it sent me spiralling into a panic

Some good luck came my way

An old friend saved the day

I thank my new friend - the mechanic

THERE WAS A LADY CALLED TRISH

There was a lady called Trish

Who wants a man who's a bit of a dish

She wants her heart stolen

By a look-a-like Marc Bolan

Instead of blokes who like taking the piss

Comedy and Darkness Poetry

A GODDESS CALLED SUE

There was a Goddess called Sue

Who is quite well to do

She isn't so shy

When she opens her third eye

She has wisdom known only by few

A LADY CALLED BRENDA

There was a lady called Brenda

Who was a really big spender

With her husband called Mick

Who she gives lots of stick

As he sings like the Great Pretender

Comedy and Darkness Poetry

A GUY CALLED MICK

There was a guy called Mick

Whose muscles were large and thick

Don't ask him to wallpaper

It turns into a caper

And his wife Brenda will feel physically sick

A GIRL CALLED CAZ

Caz thought she looked a bit sassy

You may even call her classy

She is small in height

But she can give you a fright

As she acts a little bit bad assy

Comedy and Darkness Poetry

A WOMAN CALLED SHARON

Sharon woke up with a big head lump

That turned into a rather large bump

She no longer looked cute

For her family photoshoot

She ended up looking like a chump!

MEW AND ANDREW

There was a lovely lady called Mew

Who had a good friend called Andrew

He does talks on the Solar System

You wouldn't want to miss him

You get coffee and biscuits too!

Comedy and Darkness Poetry

<u>DAWN AND HER COMEDY MANAGER</u>

Dawn met a new comedy manager
Who promised the earth if she signed her
"I'll make you a star
You will go far"
Now she can't seem to get shot of her!

Dawn met a new comedy manager
Who promised the earth if she signed her
Dawn was always provoked
At the end of her jokes
It was the comedy manager that heckled her!

Dawn met a new comedy manager
Who promised the earth if she signed her
Dawn started doing so well
With the Manager from Hell
Now Dawn can never get rid of her!

BOB THE PLUMBER

There was a plumber called Bob
Who only did half a job
He replaced my stopcock
Whilst wearing a frock
And strapping away his big knob

There was a plumber called Bob
Who only did half a job
Trading Standards were there
Whilst he changed on the stairs
And now he's just lost his job!

There was a plumber called Bob
Who ended up losing his job
He met a gangster in jail
So, he told him his tale
And he made the gangster sob!

Comedy and Darkness Poetry

There was a plumber called Bob

Who left prison and found a new job

His new gangster boyfriend

Started him on a new trend

Stealing cars with a gangster called Rob!

There was a robber called Bob

Who wanted a real proper job

He told his boyfriend

The robbing had to end

Now he wished he'd never opened his gob

There was a robber called Bob

Who finally lost his blob

He sacked his gangster boyfriend

It was a very sad end

Now he's stopped working for the mob

Comedy and Darkness Poetry

There was a guy called Bob

Who became a bit of a slob

He never worked again

He couldn't take the strain

His story could make you sob

<u>LALO AND TUCO AT THE BARISTA BOHO</u>

Two chihuahuas called Lalo and Tuco

Went to the Barista Boho

Those two naughty misfits

Ate all the doggy biscuits

Will they be allowed back? I don't know

TWO CHIHUAHUAS

I have two little chihuahuas

Who hate walks in April showers

They love a dry day

So, they can't wait for May

When they will eat all my blooming flowers!

A GUY CALLED KIRK

I knew a guy called Kirk

Who acted like a jerk

From everything that I heard

He never kept his word

This friendship will never work

Comedy and Darkness Poetry

A GIRL CALLED PAULA

There was a girl called Paula

Who never got any smaller

My dad always asked

In conversations long past

Is Paula getting any taller?

MY FRIEND CALLED MIKE

My rugby player friend called Mike

(Who liked to swim with the pike)

He has a six-foot cut out of Kylie

That makes him go rather smiley

He loves it more than his bike!

Comedy and Darkness Poetry

A GUY CALLED PETER

There was a guy called Peter

Who divorced his wife – she's a cheater

He didn't stand a chance

She was wanted by Special Branch

You really wouldn't want to meet her!

There was a man called Peter

Who couldn't pay his electric meter

He sued his ex-wife

Who caused him trouble and strife

Now he has a young wife called Nikita

Comedy and Darkness Poetry

PAULA'S DAD

I told Paula's dad *"Stop the racket"*

I think I just couldn't hack it

"Stop asking if I'm still on the shelf"

"It is worsening my mental health"

"I think you'll find I'm the shelf and the bracket!"

A DOG CALLED ROSCO

There was a dog called Rosco

Who always put on a show

If she didn't like you

She would eat your shoe

And bite all of your big toes

Comedy and Darkness Poetry

ABOUT THE POEMS

Comedy and Darkness Poetry

Comedy and Darkness Poetry

ABOUT THE POEMS

Comedy and Darkness

This poem serves as a brief introduction to the book and to my style of writing. The poem is meant to explain that I can be funny, but there is a darkness to some parts of the poetry at times.

Stealing My Socks

Still to this day, I do not understand why all the dogs I have ever owned have been obsessed with my socks. "Why are you so obsessed with my socks?" is a phrase I have said for years. It could be worse though – I could have had dogs that have run off and put puncture holes in my underwear! So, I need to be grateful for small mercies!

Clarice

This poem sprung to my mind after a phone call with my friend Dawn. She wanted to help someone out and was quite busy in her own life.

I pointed out that sometimes we cannot help everyone, and we must have time for ourselves too.

Unfortunately, we only have a finite amount of time to 'spend' our energy. Like chips in a casino, we run out eventually and sometimes we do not have the energy for ourselves. Even when we want to offer help to people, we can only do so much.

So, should we save all the lambs Clarice?

Viking Blood

This poem is dedicated to Mike who is an old schoolfriend of mine. Sometimes in life, we are too busy to acknowledge how grateful we are to have good friends who stay in our lives.

MOT Fail

This poem came after being disappointed over an MOT test of all things. It felt like there was way too much work to do on my car.

It was a reminder for me in life to not quit at the first hurdle. Things can be fixed, and you can work things out. Good friends help too!

Chrissy Rock in the Loos

A night of comedy by the legendary Chrissy Rock had me in stitches. I had to record our interaction somehow.

What better way than in a poem dedicated to her.

I have never laughed so much in ages. For some unknown reason she made a few jokes at my expense on the front row. I think my friend Dawn had something to do with it!

So, being referred to as an extra from Cocoon made my night!

A true professional and an amazing character.

The Con Man and The Lady

This is about a classic swindle based on a true story. It happened quite a while ago now to a pensioner friend of mine.

She was a tough cookie and no pushover by any means. It did leave my friend feeling ashamed by the hoodwinking of the fake 'Water Board' story, as she had not trusted her initial instincts.

She was a lady with a strong constitution. This is a warning that this kind of thing can happen to anyone.

Your Face on TV

This is for all the undesirables that keep making it onto television when they are past their sell by date. Their characters leave a lot to be desired.

Why they keep popping up in documentaries is beyond me. I got tired of certain names being mentioned all the time, so I wrote a little poem about it.

The Journey from Lanzarote

After the dark poems, I think my return journey home from a holiday should lighten the mood.

Sometimes, I think this life is one big comedy video game and I am sailing through it without a care.

I considered it a win to make an Airport Security lady from another country laugh and smile! (Even though I did run the risk of being in an episode of "Banged up Abroad".)

Coniston Lake

This poem is just one of the adventures I had in the Lake District when I was much younger. It is an unusual story that happened to me and three other friends.

I still hate dark water and I would never get in a boat again. Coniston is a lovely place, so I have been back many times.

Just not on a boat in the lake!

Comedy and Darkness Poetry

Buffalo Bill with Frosted Pink Lipstick & 10 Denier Tights

This poem is about a bizarre Wednesday night out that I experienced with workmates, to see 'The English Patient' in a cinema in Newcastle. (It was quite a long time ago now.)

I have only ever witnessed one flasher and I would not want to meet another one. He was doing more than flashing though. Maybe if I had been alone my reaction would have been different.

I could not get over the thin tights and the frosted pink lipstick. I mean, why bother?

Also, why did he have hair like Buffalo Bill from The Silence of the Lambs? Who knows.

(Obviously, I changed the police officer's name for legal reasons.)

Blake's in Town and the Killing Joker

This is a snapshot of a visit into town to a coffee shop with my good friend Ros. It is a reminder that a short conversation with a stranger can be enjoyable!

I named the waiter 'The Killing Joker' after he suggested that the book should be named 'The Killing Joke'.

This poem is also a cautionary tale to be careful chatting to me, or you could end up in a book. I might start using the phrase ***"be careful what you say or do, or you might end up in a poem or two."***

Ain't Nobody Got Time for That

This is a poem about the things that people do. You can do so much for so many people and it still does not feel good enough. No one has time to justify everything that they do for folks.

Lalo and Tuco

This poem is about two chihuahua mix dogs, named after two imaginary Mexican drug cartel dealers off the telly.

It was a Dark Damp Night

This poem was written in five minutes at the Barista Boho in North Shields on a Halloween night. A fun night was had by all!

Comedy and Darkness Poetry

Comedy and Darkness Poetry

ABOUT THE LIMERICKS

Comedy and Darkness Poetry

Comedy and Darkness Poetry

<u>ABOUT THE LIMERICKS</u>

These limericks are the light-hearted lines about people that I know. They were written to make my friends smile! I hope they make you raise an eyebrow too. Peter exists but only half of the limerick is true.

The only person that I made up was Bob the Plumber. (Although, I did once have a plumber that only did half a job with my stopcock. Plus, I do have a friend called Bob.)

Dawn

What can I say? She does drink a lot of Fanta!

Maureen

Maureen and her daughter Dawn are a double act these days! They both write good poems too.

Comedy and Darkness Poetry

A Singer called Dave

Dave exists in real life, but this is not a real lifestory. Or is it? Dave did laugh when I read this out to him!

A Guitarist called Anton

This poem was performed at the Barista Boho café. It made my night to get a few chuckles from everyone.

A Comedian called Dawn

This limerick is addressing the fact that my friend Dawn doesn't seem to think I am 'that funny'. Obviously, she is wrong. Here's hoping that this book might change her mind!

A Girl Called Carol

I put myself on the hit list!

Maraca Knacker

This limerick is based on real life, where I accidentally broke a musician's coconut maraca. I have video evidence. Luckily only one maraca was smashed, but it caused so much embarrassment.

I did apologise and offer to buy another one. It blew up in a cloud of smoke halfway through a George Michael song.

"I Gotta Have Faith" according to the busker Anton, who was singing and playing guitar at the time. I did not have any that afternoon!

The debacle entertained so many people and embarrassed the life out of me. I will never crack two maracas together again. Well, not in public anyway!

I do not know my own strength!

The Mechanic

I made a new friend when my car had its MOT done. I am so grateful to him for getting my car back on the roads!

A Lady Called Trish

This is a lovely limerick dedicated to Trish who is a lifelong Marc Bolan fan.

A Goddess Called Sue

I could not miss my friend Sue off my hit list.

A Lady Called Brenda

Brenda is a naturally hilarious lady and I had to include her husband Mick, who is also very funny!

A Guy Called Mick

This limerick was inspired by a decorating story told by my friend Mick and his wife Brenda. Let's just say don't ever ask him to decorate! It might not turn out so great!

A Girl Called Caz

An accurate description of myself! I am only joking

of course. Plus, I sometimes make people laugh.

A Woman Called Sharon

A call to wish me happy birthday inspired this limerick. Again, it is a story from real life. Poor Sharon! It was a nasty looking bite on her brow. What a lump!

Dawn and her Comedy Manager

Poor Dawn had the misfortune to be lumbered with a new comedy manager, who heckled her more than the punters did!

When asked for a comment Dawn's manager stated – ***"It's all character-building stuff, and she is amazing with hecklers now."***

Bob the Plumber

This is a fictional tale and not based on real life. (Although some parts are loosely based on real life!).

Comedy and Darkness Poetry

I wanted to do a longer set of limericks to tell a more involved story and along came my crossdressing plumber called Bob.

Lalo and Tuco at the Barista Boho

Will they stop eating all the biscuits? Who knows?

Two Chihuahuas

It comes as no surprise that my two chihuahuas hate the rain.

A Guy Called Kirk

No explanation necessary.

A Girl Called Paula

It was a running joke for years with me and my dad, that my school friend seemingly got so tall every year, whilst I didn't seem grow!

Comedy and Darkness Poetry

My Friend Called Mike

He likes a cardboard cutout. I think he took his manifestations a bit too far this time! He asked for Kylie, and he got her.

A Guy Called Peter

This is partly a true story, but I will not reveal which bits to save embarrassment!

Paula's Dad

A running theme from my friend's dad for years has been the idea of 'being left on the shelf', until one day I remarked that 'I was the shelf and I support myself!'. I haven't had any comments since!

A Dog Called Rosco

My old dog Rosco was such a character, and she is very much missed by so many people. She was fond of slippers, shoes, and toes. In that order!

Comedy and Darkness Poetry

Comedy and Darkness Poetry

OTHER BOOKS

Comedy and Darkness Poetry

Books available by Carol Monroe:

HEARTBREAK AND DARKNESS POETRY

This is a book of poetry featuring heartbreak and love poems as the central theme. Anyone going through a breakup will be able to relate to this book. Anyone not going through a breakup but can remember how it feels, will also relate to this book. It is a collection of poems that were written throughout my life.

Heartbreak and Darkness Poetry Book Quotes

"I feel immortal when I am with you!"

"Please honey tell me it's true!"

Carol Monroe

"If I could see all the stars

That shine so brightly in the sky

They would not light up my soul

Like you do"

Carol Monroe

Comedy and Darkness Poetry

I DON'T NEED YOU

I don't need a lover
I don't need a partner

I don't need someone
To make my life harder

I don't need an analyst
I don't need a shrink

I don't need a boyfriend
To make me think

Carol Monroe

Comedy and Darkness Poetry

Books available by Carol Monroe:

MENTAL HEALTH AND DARKNESS POETRY

This is a book of poetry featuring mental health as the central theme of the content. It is okay not to be okay sometimes. I live by the rules of 'if you live in the past, you will get what your past gave you.' I have always been an advocate of looking after your own mental health on a regular basis and the mental health of others.

"If you stay in the past, you will get what the past gave you. If you had a bad time, that's what you will get now."

Carol Monroe

THE THERAPIST

I went to my trauma therapist

Whose appointments I never missed

He couldn't fix my brain

Which drove him insane

Now I find myself struck off his list!

DEEP DOWN

Deep down, deeper down I'm falling

So far down, guardian angels are calling

Fight the good fight, fight hard they say

Things will change, it can't rain every day

I can't take any more of this endless darkness

In a world that seems so harsh and heartless

I am falling deep down into this awful abyss

Will I ever make it back up to the surface?

****

"You came across as a Buddhist and a mystic.

How was I to know you were covert narcissistic?"

- Carol Monroe

Comedy and Darkness Poetry

Other books available:

COMEDY, HEARTBREAK AND MENTAL HEALTH POEMS

This is a compilation of all three poetry books. However, there are no explanations of the poems at the end of the book. There are ninety poems in total to enjoy!

Comedy and Darkness Poetry

Comedy and Darkness Poetry

THE AUTHOR

Comedy and Darkness Poetry

About the Author

Carol Monroe lives in the North East of England with her two dogs, Lalo and Tuco, and has written poetry for most of her life. She has spent over 20 years taking part in local community radio stations in Newcastle upon Tyne, scripting and presenting radio shows. After performing some of her poems in local venues, she decided that a poetry book should be written and published.

She has written a comedy poetry book and another poetry book based on heartbreak, grief, and love poems, from a collection of poems penned throughout her life.

Carol has also written another poetry book based on mental health issues, including post-traumatic stress disorder, suicide, low mood, plus the effect of stalking and harassment on mental health. Her latest book is a compilation of all three poetry books which contains 90 poems altogether.

Comedy and Darkness Poetry

Printed in Great Britain
by Amazon